A Chocolate Lover's Recipe Collection

Indulge in a Variety of Mouthwatering Chocolate Treats with These Delicious Recipes

Emily Carroll

Copyright © 2023 - All rights reserved.

The content contained within this book may not be reproduced, duplicated,or transmitted without direct written permission from the author or the publisher.

Under no circumstances will any blame or legal responsibility be held againstthe publisher, or author, for any damages, reparation, or monetary loss due to the information contained within this book. Either directly or indirectly.

Legal Notice: This book is copyright protected. This book is only for personal use. You cannot amend, distribute, sell, use, quote, or paraphrase any part, or the content within this book, without the consent of the author or publisher.

Disclaimer Notice: Please note the information contained within this document is for educational and entertainment purposes only. All effort has been executed topresent accurate, up-to-date, and reliable, complete information. No warranties of any kind are declared or implied. Readers acknowledge that the author is not engaging in the rendering of legal, financial, medical, orprofessional advice. The content within this book has been derived from various sources. Please consult a licensed professional before attempting any techniques outlined in this book.

By reading this document, the reader agrees that under no circumstances is the author responsible for any losses, direct or indirect, which are incurred as a result of the use of the information contained within this document, including, but not limited to, — errors, omissions, or inaccuracies.

Table of the Contents:

Chocolate Mousse

Ingredients:

- 8 oz. bittersweet chocolate, chopped
- 1 cup heavy cream
- 3 large egg whites
- 1/4 cup granulated sugar
- 1/2 tsp vanilla extract

Instructions:

1. Melt the chocolate in a double boiler or in a microwave-safe bowl in 30-second intervals, stirring in between until smooth.
2. In a separate bowl, beat the heavy cream until stiff peaks form.
3. In another bowl, beat the egg whites until soft peaks form. Gradually add in the sugar and continue to beat until stiff peaks form.
4. Fold the melted chocolate into the whipped cream until well combined.
5. Fold in the egg white mixture until no white streaks remain.
6. Pour the mixture into individual serving dishes and refrigerate for at least 2 hours or until set.
7. Serve chilled.

Chocolate Lava Cake

Ingredients:

- 4 oz. bittersweet chocolate, chopped
- 1/2 cup unsalted butter
- 1/2 cup all-purpose flour
- 1/2 cup powdered sugar
- 2 large eggs
- 2 large egg yolks
- 1 tsp vanilla extract
- Pinch of salt
- Optional: vanilla ice cream or whipped cream for serving

Instructions:

1. Preheat the oven to 425°F (218°C). Grease four 6-ounce ramekins with butter.
2. Melt the chocolate and butter in a double boiler or in a microwave-safe bowl in 30-second intervals, stirring in between until smooth.
3. In a separate bowl, whisk together the flour and powdered sugar.
4. In another bowl, whisk together the eggs, egg yolks, vanilla extract, and salt.
5. Gradually whisk the melted chocolate mixture into the egg mixture until well combined.
6. Gradually whisk in the flour mixture until no lumps remain.
7. Divide the mixture evenly among the prepared ramekins.

8. Bake for 12-14 minutes or until the edges are set and the centers are still slightly jiggly.
9. Let cool for 1-2 minutes before running a knife around the edges and inverting onto a plate.
10. Serve immediately with vanilla ice cream or whipped cream if desired.

Chocolate Truffles

Ingredients:

- 8 oz. semisweet chocolate, chopped
- 1/2 cup heavy cream
- 1/4 cup unsalted butter, cut into small pieces
- Cocoa powder, for rolling

Instructions:

1. In a double boiler or microwave-safe bowl, melt the chocolate, heavy cream, and butter together until smooth.
2. Pour the mixture into a shallow dish and refrigerate for at least 1 hour or until firm.
3. Using a melon baller or small spoon, scoop the mixture into small balls and roll between your palms to make them smooth.
4. Roll each ball in cocoa powder to coat.

5. Serve chilled or at room temperature.

Chocolate Banana Bread Pudding

Ingredients:

- 4 cups cubed day-old bread
- 1/2 cup semisweet chocolate chips
- 2 ripe bananas, mashed
- 1/2 cup heavy cream
- 1/2 cup milk
- 2 large eggs
- 1/4 cup granulated sugar
- 1 tsp vanilla extract
- Pinch of salt

Instructions:

1. Preheat the oven to 350°F (175°C). Grease a 9-inch baking dish.
2. In a large bowl, combine the bread cubes, chocolate chips, and mashed bananas.
3. In a separate bowl, whisk together the heavy cream, milk, eggs, sugar, vanilla extract, and salt.
4. Pour the mixture over the bread mixture and stir until the bread is coated.

5. Let the mixture sit for 10-15 minutes to allow the bread
    to absorb the liquid.
6. Pour the mixture into the prepared baking dish and bake
    for 40-45 minutes or until the top is golden brown and
    the center is set.
7. Let cool for 10-15 minutes before serving.
8. Serve warm or at room temperature, optionally topped
    with whipped cream or ice cream.

Chocolate Bark

Ingredients:

- 12 oz. semisweet chocolate chips
- 1/2 cup chopped nuts (e.g. almonds, walnuts, pistachios)
- 1/2 cup dried fruit (e.g. cranberries, cherries, raisins)
- Sea salt flakes, for sprinkling

Instructions:

1. Line a baking sheet with parchment paper.
2. Melt the chocolate chips in a double boiler or
    microwave-safe bowl until smooth.
3. Pour the melted chocolate onto the prepared baking
    sheet and spread it into an even layer using a spatula.
4. Sprinkle the chopped nuts and dried fruit over the
    chocolate, pressing lightly to adhere.

5. Sprinkle sea salt flakes over the top.
6. Refrigerate for at least 1 hour or until firm.
7. Break the bark into pieces and serve.

Chocolate Dipped Fruit

Ingredients:

- Assorted fruits (e.g. strawberries, bananas, pineapple chunks)
- 8 oz. semisweet chocolate chips
- 1 tbsp coconut oil

Instructions:

1. Line a baking sheet with parchment paper.
2. Wash and dry the fruit.
3. Melt the chocolate chips and coconut oil in a double boiler or microwave-safe bowl until smooth.
4. Dip the fruit into the melted chocolate, allowing any excess to drip off.
5. Place the chocolate-coated fruit onto the prepared baking sheet.
6. Refrigerate for at least 30 minutes or until the chocolate is set.
7. Serve chilled or at room temperature.

Chocolate Fudge Brownies

Ingredients:

- 1 cup unsalted butter, melted
- 2 cups granulated sugar
- 4 large eggs
- 1 tsp vanilla extract
- 1 cup all-purpose flour
- 3/4 cup unsweetened cocoa powder
- 1/2 tsp baking powder
- 1/2 tsp salt

Instructions:

1. Preheat the oven to 350°F (175°C). Grease a 9x13 inch baking dish.
2. In a large bowl, mix together the melted butter, sugar, eggs, and vanilla extract.
3. In a separate bowl, whisk together the flour, cocoa powder, baking powder, and salt.
4. Add the dry ingredients to the wet ingredients and stir until just combined.
5. Pour the batter into the prepared baking dish and smooth the top with a spatula.
6. Bake for 25-30 minutes or until a toothpick inserted into the center comes out clean.
7. Let the brownies cool completely in the pan before slicing and serving.

Chocolate Coconut Macaroons

Ingredients:

- 2 cups sweetened shredded coconut
- 1/2 cup unsweetened cocoa powder
- 1/2 cup sweetened condensed milk
- 1/2 tsp vanilla extract
- Pinch of salt
- 2 large egg whites

Instructions:

1. Preheat the oven to 350°F (175°C). Line a baking sheet with parchment paper.
2. In a large bowl, mix together the shredded coconut, cocoa powder, sweetened condensed milk, vanilla extract, and salt.
3. In a separate bowl, beat the egg whites until stiff peaks form.
4. Fold the egg whites into the coconut mixture until well combined.
5. Using a cookie scoop or spoon, form the mixture into small mounds and place them onto the prepared baking sheet.
6. Bake for 12-15 minutes or until the macaroons are set and lightly browned.
7. Let the macaroons cool completely before serving.

Chocolate Pots de Crème

Ingredients:

- 1 1/2 cups heavy cream
- 1/2 cup whole milk
- 1/2 cup granulated sugar
- 8 oz. semisweet chocolate, finely chopped
- 6 large egg yolks
- 1 tsp vanilla extract

Instructions:

1. Preheat the oven to 325°F (160°C). Arrange six 4-ounce ramekins in a baking dish.
2. In a medium saucepan, heat the cream, milk, and sugar over medium heat, stirring occasionally, until the sugar dissolves and the mixture is hot but not boiling.
3. Remove the pan from the heat and add the chopped chocolate. Let it sit for a few minutes to melt, then whisk until smooth.
4. In a separate bowl, whisk the egg yolks and vanilla extract together.
5. Slowly pour the chocolate mixture into the egg mixture, whisking constantly.
6. Strain the mixture through a fine-mesh sieve into a large measuring cup.
7. Divide the mixture evenly among the ramekins.
8. Pour enough hot water into the baking dish to come halfway up the sides of the ramekins.

9. Bake for 30-35 minutes or until the edges are set and the centers are slightly jiggly.
10. Remove the ramekins from the water bath and let them cool to room temperature.
11. Cover and refrigerate for at least 2 hours or until chilled.
12. Serve with whipped cream or fresh berries, if desired.

Chocolate Peanut Butter Cups

Ingredients:

- 12 oz. semisweet chocolate chips
- 1/2 cup creamy peanut butter
- 2 tbsp unsalted butter, softened
- 1/4 cup powdered sugar
- 1/2 tsp vanilla extract
- Pinch of salt

Instructions:

1. Line a muffin tin with 12 paper liners.
2. Melt the chocolate chips in a double boiler or microwave-safe bowl until smooth.
3. Spoon a small amount of melted chocolate into each paper liner, using a small brush or spoon to coat the sides and bottom.

4. Refrigerate the muffin tin for 10-15 minutes or until the chocolate is set.
5. In a separate bowl, mix together the peanut butter, softened butter, powdered sugar, vanilla extract, and salt until well combined.
6. Remove the muffin tin from the refrigerator and spoon the peanut butter mixture into each cup, filling them about 3/4 of the way.
7. Spoon the remaining melted chocolate over the peanut butter mixture, using a small brush or spoon to spread it evenly and cover the top.
8. Refrigerate the muffin tin for another 10-15 minutes or until the chocolate is set.
9. Remove the peanut butter cups from the muffin tin and store them in an airtight container in the refrigerator until ready to serve.

Chocolate Caramel Tart

Ingredients: For the crust:

- 1 1/2 cups all-purpose flour
- 1/2 cup unsalted butter, cold and cut into small pieces
- 1/4 cup granulated sugar
- 1/4 tsp salt
- 1 large egg yolk
- 2 tbsp cold water

For the filling:

- 1 1/2 cups heavy cream
- 1/4 cup granulated sugar
- 6 oz. semisweet chocolate, finely chopped
- 2 tbsp unsalted butter
- 1/4 cup caramel sauce
- Pinch of salt

Instructions:

1. In a food processor, pulse together the flour, butter, sugar, and salt until the mixture resembles coarse meal.
2. Add the egg yolk and water and pulse until the dough comes together.
3. Press the dough into a 9-inch tart pan with a removable bottom. Prick the bottom with a fork and freeze for 15 minutes.
4. Preheat the oven to 375°F (190°C). Bake the crust for 20-25 minutes or until golden brown.
5. Remove the crust from the oven and let it cool completely.
6. In a medium saucepan, heat the cream and sugar over medium heat, stirring occasionally, until the sugar dissolves and the mixture is hot but not boiling.
7. Remove the pan from the heat and add the chopped chocolate and butter. Let it sit for a few minutes to melt, then whisk until smooth.
8. Stir in the caramel sauce and salt until well combined.

9. Pour the mixture into the cooled crust and smooth the top.
10. Refrigerate for at least 2 hours or until set.
11. Serve with whipped cream and chopped nuts, if desired.

Chocolate Banana Ice Cream

Ingredients:

- 3 ripe bananas, peeled and sliced
- 1/2 cup unsweetened cocoa powder
- 1/2 cup coconut milk
- 1/4 cup honey
- 1 tsp vanilla extract
- Pinch of salt

Instructions:

1. Freeze the banana slices for at least 2 hours or overnight.
2. In a blender or food processor, combine the frozen banana slices, cocoa powder, coconut milk, honey, vanilla extract, and salt.
3. Blend until smooth and creamy, scraping down the sides as needed.
4. Pour the mixture into a freezer-safe container and freeze for at least 2 hours or until firm.

5. Let the ice cream sit at room temperature for a few minutes before scooping and serving.

6. Serve with chopped nuts, whipped cream, or fresh berries, if desired.

Chocolate Almond Torte

Ingredients:

- 1 cup almond flour
- 1/2 cup all-purpose flour
- 1/2 cup granulated sugar
- 1/2 cup unsweetened cocoa powder
- 1/2 tsp baking powder
- 1/2 tsp baking soda
- 1/4 tsp salt
- 3 large eggs
- 1/2 cup unsweetened applesauce
- 1/2 cup vegetable oil
- 1 tsp vanilla extract
- 1/2 cup semisweet chocolate chips
- Sliced almonds, for topping

Instructions:

1. Preheat the oven to 350°F (175°C). Grease a 9-inch cake pan with cooking spray.
2. In a large bowl, whisk together the almond flour, all-purpose flour, sugar, cocoa powder, baking powder, baking soda, and salt.
3. In another bowl, beat the eggs, applesauce, oil, and vanilla extract until well combined.
4. Add the wet ingredients to the dry ingredients and mix until just combined.
5. Fold in the chocolate chips.
6. Pour the batter into the prepared cake pan and smooth the top with a spatula.
7. Sprinkle sliced almonds on top of the batter.
8. Bake for 25-30 minutes or until a toothpick inserted into the center comes out clean.
9. Let the torte cool in the pan for 10 minutes, then remove it from the pan and let it cool completely on a wire rack.
10. Serve with whipped cream or ice cream, if desired.

Chocolate Cherry Clafoutis

Ingredients:

- 1 cup fresh cherries, pitted and halved
- 1/4 cup granulated sugar
- 1/4 cup all-purpose flour

- 1/4 tsp salt
- 3 large eggs
- 1/2 cup whole milk
- 1/2 cup heavy cream
- 1/2 tsp vanilla extract
- 1/2 cup semisweet chocolate chips

Instructions:

1. Preheat the oven to 350°F (175°C). Grease a 9-inch pie dish with cooking spray.
2. In a small bowl, toss the cherries with 1 tbsp of sugar and set aside.
3. In a large bowl, whisk together the flour, remaining sugar, and salt.
4. In another bowl, beat the eggs, milk, cream, and vanilla extract until well combined.
5. Add the wet ingredients to the dry ingredients and whisk until smooth.
6. Fold in the chocolate chips.
7. Pour the batter into the prepared pie dish.
8. Scatter the cherries on top of the batter.
9. Bake for 30-35 minutes or until the clafoutis is puffed and golden brown.
10. Let it cool for a few minutes before serving warm or at room temperature.

Chocolate Covered Strawberries

Ingredients:

- 12-16 fresh strawberries
- 4 oz semisweet chocolate chips
- 1 tbsp coconut oil

Instructions:

1. Rinse and dry the strawberries, then set them aside.
2. In a microwave-safe bowl, melt the chocolate chips and coconut oil in 30-second intervals until fully melted and smooth.
3. Hold each strawberry by the stem and dip it into the melted chocolate until fully coated, then place it on a parchment-lined baking sheet.
4. Repeat with the remaining strawberries.
5. Let the chocolate-covered strawberries set in the fridge for at least 30 minutes, or until the chocolate is firm.
6. Serve as a sweet and simple dessert or snack.

Chocolate Chip Cookie Dough Truffles

Ingredients:

- 1/2 cup unsalted butter, at room temperature

- 1/4 cup granulated sugar
- 1/2 cup brown sugar
- 1 tsp vanilla extract
- 1 1/2 cups all-purpose flour
- 1/4 tsp salt
- 1 cup semisweet chocolate chips
- 8 oz dark chocolate, chopped
- 2 tbsp coconut oil

Instructions:

1. In a large bowl, cream together the butter, granulated sugar, brown sugar, and vanilla extract until smooth.
2. Mix in the flour and salt until well combined.
3. Fold in the chocolate chips.
4. Roll the dough into 1-inch balls and place them on a parchment-lined baking sheet.
5. Freeze the cookie dough balls for at least 30 minutes, or until firm.
6. In a microwave-safe bowl, melt the dark chocolate and coconut oil in 30-second intervals until fully melted and smooth.
7. Using a fork or toothpick, dip each cookie dough ball into the melted chocolate until fully coated, then place it back on the parchment-lined baking sheet.
8. Repeat with the remaining cookie dough balls.
9. Let the chocolate-covered truffles set in the fridge for at least 30 minutes, or until the chocolate is firm.
10. Serve as a decadent and indulgent dessert or gift.

Chocolate Orange Tart

Ingredients:

- 1 1/2 cups all-purpose flour
- 1/2 cup unsalted butter, chilled and cubed
- 1/4 cup granulated sugar
- 1/4 cup cocoa powder
- 1/2 tsp salt
- 1 large egg
- 1/4 cup heavy cream
- 1/4 cup orange marmalade
- 8 oz dark chocolate, chopped
- 1/2 cup heavy cream, for ganache

Instructions:

1. Preheat the oven to 350°F.
2. In a food processor, combine flour, butter, sugar, cocoa powder, and salt until it forms a crumbly mixture.
3. Add egg and heavy cream and pulse until the dough comes together.
4. Press the dough into a 9-inch tart pan and prick the bottom with a fork.
5. Bake for 20-25 minutes until the crust is set.
6. In a small saucepan, heat marmalade until it becomes liquid, then brush the bottom of the crust with it.
7. In another saucepan, heat heavy cream until it begins to steam, then pour over the chopped chocolate. Let it sit for a few minutes, then whisk until smooth.

8. Pour the chocolate ganache into the crust and chill in the refrigerator for at least 2 hours.

Dark Chocolate Panna Cotta

Ingredients:

- 1/4 cup cold water
- 1 envelope unflavored gelatin
- 2 cups heavy cream
- 1/2 cup granulated sugar
- 1/2 tsp salt
- 6 oz dark chocolate, chopped
- 1 tsp vanilla extract
- Fresh berries, for garnish

Instructions:

1. In a small bowl, sprinkle gelatin over cold water and let it sit for 5 minutes.
2. In a saucepan, heat cream, sugar, and salt until it begins to steam.
3. Add the chopped chocolate and vanilla extract, and stir until the chocolate is melted and the mixture is smooth.
4. Add the gelatin mixture and whisk until fully dissolved.

5. Pour the mixture into 4-6 ramekins and refrigerate for at least 4 hours or overnight.
6. To serve, run a knife around the edge of each ramekin and invert onto a plate. Garnish with fresh berries.

Chocolate Tiramisu

Ingredients:

- 6 egg yolks
- 1 cup granulated sugar
- 1/2 cup unsweetened cocoa powder
- 1/4 cup strong brewed coffee
- 2 cups heavy cream
- 1 tsp vanilla extract
- 24 ladyfingers
- 1/2 cup semisweet chocolate chips, for garnish

Instructions:

1. In a heatproof bowl, whisk together egg yolks, sugar, cocoa powder, and coffee.
2. Place the bowl over a pot of simmering water and whisk continuously until the mixture thickens and doubles in volume.
3. Remove the bowl from the heat and let it cool to room temperature.

4. In a separate bowl, whip heavy cream and vanilla extract until it forms stiff peaks.

5. Fold the whipped cream into the chocolate mixture until fully incorporated.

6. Dip ladyfingers in coffee and arrange them in a single layer in a 9x13 inch dish.

7. Spread half of the chocolate mixture over the ladyfingers.

8. Repeat with another layer of soaked ladyfingers and the remaining chocolate mixture.

9. Cover and chill in the refrigerator for at least 2 hours.

10. Before serving, sprinkle chocolate chips over the top.

Chocolate Hazelnut Tart

Ingredients:

- 1 1/2 cups all-purpose flour
- 1/2 cup unsalted butter, chilled and cubed
- 1/4 cup granulated sugar
- 1/4 tsp salt
- 2 cups hazelnuts, toasted and chopped
- 1/2 cup semisweet chocolate chips
- 1/2 cup heavy cream
- 1/4 cup hazelnut spread

Instructions:

1. Preheat the oven to 350°F.
2. In a food processor, combine flour, butter, sugar, and salt until it forms a crumbly mixture.
3. Press the dough into a 9-inch tart pan and prick the bottom with a fork.
4. Bake for 20-25 minutes until the crust is set.
5. In a small saucepan, heat hazelnut spread and heavy cream until it becomes a smooth mixture.
6. In a bowl, mix together chopped hazelnuts and chocolate chips.
7. Pour the hazelnut spread mixture over the bottom of the crust.
8. Sprinkle the hazelnut and chocolate mixture over the top.
9. Bake for an additional 10-15 minutes until the chocolate is melted and the nuts are toasted.
10. Let the tart cool to room temperature before serving.

Chocolate Meringue Pie

Ingredients:

- 1 pie crust, pre-baked
- 4 egg whites

- 1 cup granulated sugar
- 1/4 cup unsweetened cocoa powder
- 1 tsp white vinegar
- 1 tsp vanilla extract
- 1 cup semisweet chocolate chips

Instructions:

1. Preheat the oven to 350°F.
2. In a large mixing bowl, beat egg whites until they form stiff peaks.
3. Gradually add sugar, cocoa powder, vinegar, and vanilla extract to the egg whites, beating well after each addition.
4. Fold in chocolate chips.
5. Pour the mixture into the pre-baked pie crust.
6. Bake for 25-30 minutes until the meringue is golden brown.
7. Allow the pie to cool before serving.

Chocolate Avocado Pudding

Ingredients:

- 2 ripe avocados, peeled and pitted
- 1/2 cup unsweetened cocoa powder
- 1/2 cup maple syrup
- 1/2 cup almond milk

- 1 tsp vanilla extract
- 1/4 tsp salt

Instructions:

1. In a food processor or blender, puree the avocados until smooth.
2. Add cocoa powder, maple syrup, almond milk, vanilla extract, and salt, and blend until fully combined.
3. Divide the mixture into serving dishes and chill for at least 30 minutes before serving.
4. Optional: Top with whipped cream or shaved chocolate before serving.

Chocolate Raspberry Tart

Ingredients:

- 1 pie crust, pre-baked
- 1 cup semisweet chocolate chips
- 1/2 cup heavy cream
- 1 tbsp unsalted butter
- 1/4 cup raspberry jam
- 1 pint fresh raspberries

Instructions:

1. In a medium saucepan, melt the chocolate chips, heavy cream, and butter over low heat.
2. Once melted, pour the mixture into the pre-baked pie crust and spread it evenly.
3. In a small bowl, microwave the raspberry jam for 30 seconds or until melted.
4. Spoon the melted jam over the chocolate mixture and spread it evenly.
5. Top the tart with fresh raspberries.
6. Chill in the fridge for at least 1 hour before serving.

Chocolate and Peanut Butter Rice Krispie Treats

Ingredients:

- 3 tbsp unsalted butter
- 1 package (10 oz) mini marshmallows
- 6 cups Rice Krispies cereal
- 1 cup semisweet chocolate chips
- 1/2 cup creamy peanut butter

Instructions:

1. In a large pot, melt the butter over low heat.
2. Add the mini marshmallows to the pot and stir until melted.

3. Remove the pot from the heat and add the Rice Krispies cereal. Mix until the cereal is fully coated.
4. Transfer the mixture into a greased 9x13 inch baking dish and press it down evenly.
5. In a small saucepan, melt the chocolate chips and peanut butter over low heat.
6. Once melted, pour the mixture over the Rice Krispie treats and spread it evenly.
7. Chill in the fridge for at least 1 hour before slicing and serving.

Chocolate Espresso Mousse

Ingredients:

- 1/2 cup semisweet chocolate chips
- 2 tbsp unsalted butter
- 2 tbsp brewed espresso
- 1/4 tsp vanilla extract
- 1/2 cup heavy cream
- 1 egg white
- 1 tbsp granulated sugar

Instructions:

1. In a medium saucepan, melt the chocolate chips and butter over low heat.

2. Once melted, remove the pan from the heat and stir in the brewed espresso and vanilla extract.
3. In a separate bowl, whip the heavy cream until it forms stiff peaks.
4. In another bowl, beat the egg white until it forms soft peaks. Gradually add the granulated sugar and continue beating until it forms stiff peaks.
5. Fold the whipped cream into the chocolate mixture until well combined.
6. Gently fold the beaten egg white into the chocolate mixture until just combined.
7. Pour the mousse into individual serving dishes and chill in the fridge for at least 1 hour before serving.

Chocolate Oreo Cheesecake Bars

Ingredients:

- 24 Oreo cookies
- 1/4 cup unsalted butter, melted
- 16 oz cream cheese, softened
- 1/2 cup granulated sugar
- 1 tsp vanilla extract
- 2 eggs
- 1 cup semisweet chocolate chips, melted

Instructions:

1. Preheat the oven to 325°F (160°C) and line an 8x8 inch baking pan with parchment paper.
2. Crush the Oreo cookies into fine crumbs and mix with the melted butter. Press the mixture into the bottom of the prepared baking pan.
3. In a large bowl, beat the cream cheese until smooth.
4. Add the granulated sugar and vanilla extract and continue beating until well combined.
5. Beat in the eggs one at a time until fully incorporated.
6. Pour the cheesecake mixture over the Oreo crust and smooth it out evenly.
7. Drizzle the melted chocolate over the cheesecake mixture and use a knife to swirl it into the batter.
8. Bake for 35-40 minutes or until the cheesecake is set.
9. Let the cheesecake cool to room temperature before chilling in the fridge for at least 2 hours.
10. Cut into bars and serve.

Chocolate Mint Brownies

Ingredients:

- 1 cup butter
- 2 cups sugar
- 4 eggs

- 1 tsp vanilla extract
- 1/2 tsp peppermint extract
- 1 1/3 cups flour
- 3/4 cup cocoa powder
- 1/2 tsp baking powder
- 1/2 tsp salt
- 1 cup chocolate chips
- 1/2 cup chopped walnuts (optional)

Instructions:

1. Preheat oven to 350°F (175°C).
2. Melt butter in a large saucepan over low heat. Remove from heat and stir in sugar, eggs, vanilla extract, and peppermint extract.
3. In a separate bowl, whisk together flour, cocoa powder, baking powder, and salt.
4. Gradually stir the dry ingredients into the butter mixture until well combined.
5. Fold in the chocolate chips and chopped walnuts (if using).
6. Pour the batter into a greased 9x13 inch baking pan.
7. Bake for 25-30 minutes, or until a toothpick inserted in the center comes out clean.
8. Allow the brownies to cool before cutting into squares and serving.

Triple Chocolate Cheesecake

Ingredients:

- 1 1/2 cups chocolate cookie crumbs
- 1/4 cup unsalted butter, melted
- 3 (8 oz) packages cream cheese, softened
- 1 cup sugar
- 1 tsp vanilla extract
- 3 eggs
- 1/2 cup semisweet chocolate chips, melted
- 1/2 cup white chocolate chips, melted
- 1/2 cup milk chocolate chips, melted

Instructions:

1. Preheat oven to 350°F (175°C).
2. In a medium bowl, mix together the chocolate cookie crumbs and melted butter. Press the mixture into the bottom of a 9-inch springform pan.
3. In a large bowl, beat the cream cheese until smooth.
4. Gradually add in the sugar and vanilla extract, beating until well combined.
5. Beat in the eggs, one at a time, until fully incorporated.
6. Divide the cheesecake batter into three separate bowls.
7. Stir the melted semisweet chocolate chips into one bowl of batter, the melted white chocolate chips into another bowl of batter, and the melted milk chocolate chips into the remaining bowl of batter.

8. Pour the three batters into the prepared crust in any order you prefer.
9. Bake for 45-50 minutes, or until the center is almost set.
10. Allow the cheesecake to cool to room temperature before refrigerating for at least 4 hours or overnight.
11. Serve chilled.

Chocolate and Pistachio Tart

Ingredients:

- 1 1/2 cups all-purpose flour
- 1/2 cup unsalted butter, chilled and cut into small pieces
- 1/2 cup granulated sugar
- 1/4 cup cocoa powder
- 1/4 teaspoon salt
- 1/2 cup semisweet chocolate chips
- 1/2 cup heavy cream
- 1/4 cup unsalted pistachios, chopped

Instructions:

1. Preheat the oven to 350°F.
2. In a large mixing bowl, combine the flour, butter, sugar, cocoa powder, and salt. Mix well until the mixture is crumbly.

3. Press the mixture into a 9-inch tart pan with a removable bottom. Make sure to press the mixture up the sides of the pan as well.
4. Bake the crust for 12-15 minutes, or until set. Remove from the oven and let it cool completely.
5. In a small saucepan, heat the heavy cream until it just begins to simmer.
6. Remove the cream from the heat and add the chocolate chips. Whisk until the chocolate is melted and the mixture is smooth.
7. Pour the chocolate mixture into the cooled tart crust and smooth it out with a spatula.
8. Sprinkle the chopped pistachios on top of the chocolate filling.
9. Refrigerate the tart for at least 1 hour, or until the chocolate filling is set.
10. Serve and enjoy!

Chocolate and Cherry Clafoutis

Ingredients:

- 1 cup all-purpose flour
- 1/2 cup granulated sugar
- 1/4 teaspoon salt
- 4 large eggs
- 1 1/4 cups milk

- 1 teaspoon vanilla extract
- 1/2 cup semisweet chocolate chips
- 1 cup fresh cherries, pitted

Instructions:

1. Preheat the oven to 375°F.
2. In a large mixing bowl, combine the flour, sugar, and salt. Mix well.
3. In another bowl, whisk together the eggs, milk, and vanilla extract.
4. Add the egg mixture to the flour mixture and whisk until smooth.
5. Stir in the chocolate chips.
6. Pour the batter into a greased 9-inch pie dish.
7. Scatter the cherries evenly on top of the batter.
8. Bake the clafoutis for 30-35 minutes, or until golden brown and set in the middle.
9. Remove from the oven and let it cool for a few minutes.
10. Slice and serve warm or at room temperature.

Chocolate Cherry Cheesecake Bars

Ingredients:

- 1 1/2 cups graham cracker crumbs
- 1/4 cup sugar
- 1/2 cup butter, melted
- 1 1/2 cups semisweet chocolate chips
- 1 can cherry pie filling
- 2 packages cream cheese, softened
- 1/2 cup sugar
- 2 eggs
- 1 tsp vanilla extract

Directions:

1. Preheat the oven to 350°F (175°C).
2. In a bowl, combine the graham cracker crumbs, sugar, and melted butter. Press the mixture into the bottom of a 9x13 inch baking pan.
3. Sprinkle the chocolate chips over the crust, then spoon the cherry pie filling over the chocolate chips.
4. In another bowl, beat the cream cheese, sugar, eggs, and vanilla extract together until smooth. Pour the mixture over the cherry pie filling.
5. Bake for 35-40 minutes or until the cheesecake is set. Cool before cutting into bars.

Chocolate and Hazelnut Pudding

Ingredients:

- 1/2 cup sugar
- 1/4 cup cornstarch
- 1/4 cup unsweetened cocoa powder
- 1/4 tsp salt
- 3 cups milk
- 3 egg yolks, beaten
- 2 tbsp butter
- 1 tsp vanilla extract
- 1/2 cup chopped hazelnuts
- Whipped cream, for topping

Directions:

1. In a medium saucepan, whisk together the sugar, cornstarch, cocoa powder, and salt. Gradually whisk in the milk until smooth.
2. Cook over medium heat, whisking constantly, until the mixture thickens and comes to a boil. Boil for 1 minute, whisking constantly.
3. Remove the pan from the heat. Gradually whisk about 1 cup of the hot mixture into the beaten egg yolks, then whisk the egg mixture back into the pan.
4. Cook over medium heat, whisking constantly, until the mixture thickens and comes to a boil again. Boil for 1 minute, whisking constantly.

5. Remove the pan from the heat and stir in the butter, vanilla extract, and chopped hazelnuts. Pour the pudding into individual serving dishes.
6. Cover the dishes with plastic wrap and chill in the refrigerator for at least 2 hours or until set.
7. Top with whipped cream before serving.

Chocolate Stout Cake

Ingredients:

- 1 cup unsalted butter, softened
- 2 cups granulated sugar
- 4 large eggs
- 2 teaspoons vanilla extract
- 1 1/4 cups all-purpose flour
- 3/4 cup unsweetened cocoa powder
- 1 teaspoon baking soda
- 1/2 teaspoon baking powder
- 1/2 teaspoon salt
- 1 cup stout beer
- 1/2 cup sour cream

Instructions:

1. Preheat the oven to 350°F. Grease and flour a 9-inch round cake pan.

2. In a large bowl, cream together the butter and sugar until light and fluffy.
3. Beat in the eggs one at a time, then stir in the vanilla.
4. In a separate bowl, sift together the flour, cocoa powder, baking soda, baking powder, and salt.
5. Gradually add the dry ingredients to the butter mixture, alternating with the stout beer and sour cream.
6. Pour the batter into the prepared pan and bake for 45-50 minutes, or until a toothpick inserted in the center comes out clean.
7. Let the cake cool in the pan for 10 minutes before transferring to a wire rack to cool completely.
8. Serve with whipped cream or chocolate ganache, if desired.

Chocolate Mascarpone Tart

Ingredients:

- 1 1/2 cups all-purpose flour
- 1/4 cup granulated sugar
- 1/4 teaspoon salt
- 1/2 cup unsalted butter, chilled and cubed
- 1 egg yolk
- 8 ounces mascarpone cheese, softened
- 1/2 cup heavy cream

- 8 ounces semisweet chocolate, chopped
- 1/2 teaspoon vanilla extract

Instructions:

1. Preheat the oven to 375°F. Grease a 9-inch tart pan with a removable bottom.
2. In a food processor, pulse together the flour, sugar, and salt.
3. Add the butter and pulse until the mixture resembles coarse sand.
4. Add the egg yolk and pulse until the dough comes together.
5. Press the dough into the prepared tart pan and prick the bottom all over with a fork.
6. Bake for 15-20 minutes, or until golden brown. Let cool completely.
7. In a small saucepan, heat the heavy cream until just simmering.
8. Remove from heat and add the chopped chocolate. Stir until smooth and melted.
9. In a large bowl, whisk together the mascarpone cheese and vanilla extract.
10. Pour the chocolate mixture into the bowl and whisk until well combined.
11. Pour the mixture into the cooled tart shell and smooth the top.
12. Refrigerate for at least 2 hours, or until set.
13. Serve with whipped cream and fresh berries, if desired.

Chocolate Covered Pretzel Torte

Ingredients:

- 2 cups pretzels, crushed
- 1/2 cup unsalted butter, melted
- 1/4 cup granulated sugar
- 1/4 cup cocoa powder
- 1/4 cup heavy cream
- 12 ounces semisweet chocolate, chopped
- 4 large eggs
- 1/2 cup granulated sugar
- 1/2 cup all-purpose flour
- 1/2 teaspoon salt
- 1/2 teaspoon baking powder

Instructions:

1. Preheat the oven to 350°F. Grease a 9-inch springform pan.
2. In a bowl, combine the crushed pretzels, melted butter, and 1/4 cup sugar. Press the mixture into the bottom of the prepared pan.
3. In a small saucepan, heat the heavy cream until just simmering.
4. Remove from heat and add the chopped chocolate. Stir until smooth and melted.
5. In a large bowl, beat the eggs and 1/2 cup sugar until light and fluffy.

6. In a separate bowl, whisk together the flour, cocoa powder, salt, and baking powder.
7. Gradually add the dry ingredients to the egg mixture, stirring until just combined.
8. Pour the chocolate mixture into the batter and fold until fully combined.
9. Pour the batter into the prepared pan and bake for 30-35 minutes, or until a toothpick inserted in the center comes out clean.
10. Let the cake cool in the pan for 10 minutes before transferring to a wire rack to cool completely.
11. Serve with whipped cream and chocolate-covered pretzels.

Chocolate Cheesecake Bars with Raspberries

Ingredients:

- 1 cup graham cracker crumbs
- 1/4 cup unsalted butter, melted
- 1/4 cup granulated sugar
- 12 ounces semisweet chocolate, chopped
- 2 (8-ounce) packages cream cheese, softened
- 1/2 cup granulated sugar
- 2 large eggs
- 1/2 teaspoon vanilla extract

- 1 cup fresh raspberries

Instructions:

1. Preheat the oven to 350°F. Grease an 8-inch square baking pan.
2. In a bowl, combine the graham cracker crumbs, melted butter, and 1/4 cup sugar. Press the mixture into the bottom of the prepared pan.
3. In a small saucepan, heat the chopped chocolate until just melted. Set aside to cool slightly.
4. In a large bowl, beat the cream cheese and 1/2 cup sugar until light and fluffy.
5. Add the eggs one at a time, beating well after each addition.
6. Stir in the vanilla extract and melted chocolate.
7. Pour the cheesecake mixture over the graham cracker crust.
8. Dot the raspberries over the top of the cheesecake mixture.
9. Bake for 30-35 minutes, or until the edges are set and the center is slightly jiggly.
10. Let the cheesecake cool in the pan for 10 minutes before transferring to a wire rack to cool completely.
11. Chill in the refrigerator for at least 2 hours before serving.

Chocolate Bread Pudding with Whiskey Sauce

Ingredients:

- 1 loaf of French bread, cut into 1-inch cubes
- 2 cups of milk
- 2 cups of heavy cream
- 1 cup of sugar
- 1/2 cup of unsweetened cocoa powder
- 4 large eggs
- 2 teaspoons of vanilla extract
- 1/2 teaspoon of salt
- 1/2 cup of semisweet chocolate chips
- 1/2 cup of chopped pecans
- 1/2 cup of whiskey
- 1/2 cup of unsalted butter

Instructions:

1. Preheat the oven to 350°F.
2. In a large bowl, whisk together the milk, heavy cream, sugar, cocoa powder, eggs, vanilla extract, and salt.
3. Add the bread cubes to the mixture and toss to coat.
4. Fold in the chocolate chips and pecans.
5. Pour the mixture into a greased 9x13 inch baking dish.
6. Bake for 45-50 minutes, or until the bread pudding is set.
7. Meanwhile, in a small saucepan, heat the whiskey and butter over medium heat until the butter is melted.
8. Serve the bread pudding warm with the whiskey sauce.

Chocolate Peanut Butter Banana Bites

Ingredients:

- 2 ripe bananas, sliced into 1/2 inch rounds
- 1/4 cup of creamy peanut butter
- 1/4 cup of semisweet chocolate chips
- 1 teaspoon of coconut oil

Instructions:

1. Line a baking sheet with parchment paper.
2. Spread a small amount of peanut butter on top of each banana slice.
3. Place another banana slice on top to make a sandwich.
4. Place the banana sandwiches on the prepared baking sheet and freeze for at least 1 hour.
5. In a small microwave-safe bowl, combine the chocolate chips and coconut oil.
6. Microwave in 30-second intervals, stirring between each, until the chocolate is melted and smooth.
7. Remove the banana sandwiches from the freezer and dip them halfway into the melted chocolate.
8. Place the bites back on the parchment paper and freeze for another 30 minutes, or until the chocolate is set.

Chocolate Hazelnut Cake Roll

Ingredients:

- 4 large eggs
- 1/2 cup granulated sugar
- 1/4 cup all-purpose flour
- 1/4 cup unsweetened cocoa powder
- 1/2 teaspoon baking powder
- 1/4 teaspoon salt
- 1 cup Nutella or chocolate hazelnut spread
- 1 cup heavy cream
- 1 teaspoon vanilla extract
- Powdered sugar for dusting

Instructions:

1. Preheat oven to 350°F. Line a 15x10x1-inch jelly roll pan with parchment paper.
2. In a large bowl, beat the eggs and sugar with an electric mixer on high speed for 5 minutes or until thick and pale yellow.
3. In a separate bowl, whisk together the flour, cocoa powder, baking powder, and salt. Gradually fold the dry mixture into the egg mixture until just combined.
4. Pour the batter into the prepared pan and smooth it out evenly.
5. Bake for 12-15 minutes or until the cake springs back when lightly touched.

6. Immediately after removing the cake from the oven, invert it onto a clean kitchen towel that has been sprinkled with powdered sugar. Peel off the parchment paper.
7. Starting at the short end, roll up the cake and towel together. Let it cool completely in the rolled position.
8. In a large bowl, beat the Nutella, heavy cream, and vanilla extract until light and fluffy.
9. Carefully unroll the cooled cake and spread the Nutella mixture over the top, leaving a 1-inch border on all sides.
10. Gently roll the cake back up, starting with the short end and using the towel to help you roll it.
11. Place the cake roll seam-side down on a serving plate and dust with powdered sugar. Chill for at least 1 hour before slicing and serving.

Chocolate Covered Cherry Cheesecake Bites

Ingredients:

- 1 package (8 ounces) cream cheese, softened
- 1/2 cup granulated sugar
- 1 egg
- 1 teaspoon vanilla extract
- 1 cup semisweet chocolate chips
- 1 tablespoon shortening

- 24 maraschino cherries with stems, drained and patted dry

Instructions:

1. Preheat oven to 350°F. Line a 24-cup mini muffin tin with paper liners.
2. In a medium bowl, beat the cream cheese, sugar, egg, and vanilla extract until smooth.
3. Spoon the cream cheese mixture into the prepared muffin cups, filling each one about 2/3 full.
4. Bake for 12-15 minutes or until the edges are lightly golden and the centers are set.
5. Let the cheesecakes cool completely in the pan before removing them to a wire rack.
6. In a small saucepan, melt the chocolate chips and shortening over low heat, stirring constantly until smooth.
7. Dip each cherry into the chocolate mixture and place it on top of a cheesecake.
8. Drizzle any remaining chocolate over the cheesecakes.
9. Chill in the refrigerator for at least 30 minutes or until the chocolate is set. Serve chilled.

Chocolate Covered Strawberry Cake

Ingredients:

- 1 1/2 cups all-purpose flour
- 3/4 cup unsweetened cocoa powder
- 1 1/2 teaspoons baking powder
- 1 teaspoon baking soda
- 1/2 teaspoon salt
- 1 cup sugar
- 2 large eggs
- 1/2 cup vegetable oil
- 1/2 cup whole milk
- 1/2 cup boiling water
- 1 cup fresh strawberries, sliced
- 1 cup semisweet chocolate chips

Instructions:

1. Preheat the oven to 350°F. Grease and flour a 9-inch cake pan.
2. In a medium bowl, whisk together the flour, cocoa powder, baking powder, baking soda, and salt.
3. In a separate large bowl, whisk together the sugar, eggs, and vegetable oil until well combined.
4. Add half of the dry ingredients to the wet ingredients and whisk until just combined. Then add the remaining dry ingredients and whisk until just combined.
5. Add the whole milk and whisk until smooth.

6. Gradually whisk in the boiling water until the batter is smooth.
7. Stir in the sliced strawberries and chocolate chips.
8. Pour the batter into the prepared cake pan and bake for 35-40 minutes, or until a toothpick inserted into the center of the cake comes out clean.
9. Let the cake cool completely in the pan before removing and serving.

Chocolate Pecan Pie Bars

Ingredients:

- 2 cups all-purpose flour
- 1/2 cup granulated sugar
- 1/2 teaspoon salt
- 3/4 cup unsalted butter, chilled and cubed
- 2 large eggs
- 1/2 cup dark corn syrup
- 1/2 cup light brown sugar, packed
- 1/4 cup unsweetened cocoa powder
- 1/4 cup unsalted butter, melted
- 1 teaspoon vanilla extract
- 1 1/2 cups pecans, chopped
- 1/2 cup semisweet chocolate chips

Instructions:

1. Preheat the oven to 350°F. Grease a 9x13 inch baking dish.
2. In a large bowl, whisk together the flour, granulated sugar, and salt.
3. Using a pastry blender, cut in the chilled butter until the mixture resembles coarse crumbs.
4. Press the mixture into the prepared baking dish and bake for 20 minutes.
5. In a medium bowl, whisk together the eggs, corn syrup, brown sugar, cocoa powder, melted butter, and vanilla extract.
6. Stir in the chopped pecans and chocolate chips.
7. Pour the filling over the warm crust and spread it evenly.
8. Bake for 25-30 minutes, or until the filling is set.
9. Let the bars cool completely in the pan before cutting into squares and serving.

Chocolate Banana Brownie Bites

Ingredients:

- 2 ripe bananas
- 1/2 cup almond flour
- 1/4 cup cocoa powder
- 1/4 cup maple syrup

- 1/4 cup chocolate chips
- 1/4 tsp salt
- 1/4 tsp baking powder

Directions:

1. Preheat oven to 350°F (180°C). Grease a mini muffin tin.
2. In a mixing bowl, mash the bananas until smooth.
3. Add almond flour, cocoa powder, maple syrup, salt, and baking powder to the mixing bowl. Mix until smooth.
4. Add chocolate chips to the mixing bowl and stir until combined.
5. Scoop the batter into the prepared mini muffin tin and bake for 12-15 minutes.
6. Let cool for a few minutes before removing from the muffin tin.

Chocolate Coconut Pudding

Ingredients:

- 1 can full-fat coconut milk
- 1/2 cup cocoa powder
- 1/4 cup maple syrup
- 1 tsp vanilla extract
- 1/4 tsp salt

Directions:

1. In a medium saucepan, heat coconut milk over medium heat.
2. Add cocoa powder, maple syrup, vanilla extract, and salt to the saucepan. Whisk until smooth.
3. Continue to heat the mixture, whisking occasionally, until it thickens and coats the back of a spoon, about 10-15 minutes.
4. Remove the saucepan from heat and let cool for a few minutes.
5. Pour the pudding into small jars or ramekins and refrigerate for at least 2 hours before serving.

Chocolate Hazelnut Biscotti

Ingredients:

- 1/2 cup unsalted butter, softened
- 3/4 cup granulated sugar
- 2 large eggs
- 1 tsp vanilla extract
- 1 3/4 cups all-purpose flour
- 1/4 cup unsweetened cocoa powder
- 1 tsp baking powder
- 1/2 tsp salt

- 1 cup chopped hazelnuts
- 1/2 cup semisweet chocolate chips

Instructions:

1. Preheat oven to 350°F (180°C). Line a baking sheet with parchment paper.
2. In a large bowl, cream the butter and sugar together until light and fluffy.
3. Add the eggs and vanilla extract, and mix well.
4. In a separate bowl, whisk together the flour, cocoa powder, baking powder, and salt.
5. Gradually add the dry ingredients to the butter mixture, mixing until just combined.
6. Stir in the chopped hazelnuts and chocolate chips.
7. Form the dough into two logs on the prepared baking sheet.
8. Bake for 25-30 minutes or until the logs are firm to the touch.
9. Let the logs cool for 10 minutes, then use a serrated knife to slice them into 1/2-inch-thick slices.
10. Place the slices back on the baking sheet and bake for another 15-20 minutes, or until the biscotti are crisp and dry.

Chocolate Cheesecake Brownies

Ingredients:

- 1 box brownie mix
- 1/2 cup vegetable oil
- 1/4 cup water
- 2 large eggs
- 8 oz cream cheese, softened
- 1/4 cup granulated sugar
- 1 large egg yolk
- 1 tsp vanilla extract
- 1/2 cup semisweet chocolate chips

Instructions:

1. Preheat oven to 350°F (180°C). Grease a 9x13 inch baking dish.
2. In a large bowl, mix together the brownie mix, oil, water, and eggs until well combined.
3. Pour the brownie batter into the prepared baking dish.
4. In a separate bowl, beat the cream cheese, sugar, egg yolk, and vanilla extract together until smooth.
5. Fold in the chocolate chips.
6. Pour the cheesecake mixture on top of the brownie batter. Use a knife to swirl the two batters together.
7. Bake for 35-40 minutes or until a toothpick inserted in the center comes out clean.

8. Let the brownies cool completely before cutting into squares.

Chocolate Caramel Tartlets

Ingredients:

- 1 cup all-purpose flour
- 1/4 cup cocoa powder
- 1/4 cup sugar
- 1/2 cup unsalted butter, cold and cubed
- 1/4 cup caramel sauce
- 1/2 cup dark chocolate chips
- 1/4 cup heavy cream

Instructions:

1. Preheat the oven to 350°F (175°C).
2. In a bowl, mix the flour, cocoa powder, and sugar.
3. Cut in the butter using a pastry blender or your fingers until the mixture resembles coarse sand.
4. Press the mixture into the bottom and up the sides of four tartlet pans.
5. Bake the crusts for 10-12 minutes or until they are set.
6. Let them cool.

7. In a saucepan over low heat, combine the caramel sauce and dark chocolate chips.
8. Stir until the chocolate is melted and the mixture is smooth.
9. Remove from heat and add the heavy cream, stirring until well combined.
10. Pour the chocolate mixture into the cooled crusts.
11. Refrigerate for 30 minutes or until the chocolate has set.
12. Serve and enjoy!

Chocolate Chia Seed Pudding

Ingredients:

- 1/4 cup chia seeds
- 1 1/2 cups almond milk
- 1/4 cup cocoa powder
- 2-3 tablespoons honey or maple syrup
- 1/2 teaspoon vanilla extract

Instructions:

1. In a bowl, whisk together the chia seeds, almond milk, cocoa powder, sweetener of your choice, and vanilla extract.
2. Pour the mixture into a jar with a tight-fitting lid.

3. Shake the jar well to ensure that the chia seeds are evenly distributed.
4. Refrigerate for at least 4 hours or overnight.
5. Stir well before serving.
6. Top with fresh berries, chopped nuts, or whipped cream if desired.
7. Serve and enjoy!

Chocolate Toffee Crunch Bars

Ingredients:

- 1 cup all-purpose flour
- 1/2 cup unsweetened cocoa powder
- 1/2 cup granulated sugar
- 1/2 cup unsalted butter, melted
- 1 cup semi-sweet chocolate chips
- 1 cup toffee bits
- 1/2 cup sweetened condensed milk

Instructions:

1. Preheat the oven to 350°F (180°C). Grease an 8-inch square baking pan.
2. In a medium bowl, whisk together the flour, cocoa powder, and sugar.
3. Add the melted butter and mix until well combined.

4. Press the mixture into the prepared pan.
5. Bake for 15 minutes.
6. Sprinkle the chocolate chips and toffee bits over the top.
7. Drizzle the sweetened condensed milk over the chocolate chips and toffee bits.
8. Bake for an additional 15-20 minutes, or until the edges are lightly browned and the chocolate chips are melted.
9. Let cool completely in the pan before cutting into bars.

Chocolate Chip Cookie Dough Cheesecake Bars

Ingredients:

- 1 1/2 cups graham cracker crumbs
- 1/4 cup granulated sugar
- 1/2 cup unsalted butter, melted
- 16 oz cream cheese, softened
- 1/2 cup granulated sugar
- 2 large eggs
- 1 tsp vanilla extract
- 1/2 cup all-purpose flour
- 1/2 cup mini chocolate chips

Instructions:

1. Preheat the oven to 350°F (180°C). Grease an 8-inch square baking pan.
2. In a medium bowl, mix together the graham cracker crumbs, 1/4 cup sugar, and melted butter.
3. Press the mixture into the prepared pan.
4. In a large bowl, beat the cream cheese and 1/2 cup sugar until smooth.
5. Beat in the eggs and vanilla.
6. Mix in the flour until well combined.
7. Stir in the mini chocolate chips.
8. Pour the mixture over the crust.
9. Bake for 30-35 minutes, or until the edges are lightly browned and the center is set.
10. Let cool completely in the pan before cutting into bars.

Chocolate Soufflé

Ingredients:

- 4 oz semisweet chocolate, chopped
- 3 tbsp unsalted butter, plus more for greasing ramekins
- 3 tbsp all-purpose flour
- 1/2 cup whole milk
- 2 large eggs, separated
- 1/4 cup granulated sugar, plus more for dusting ramekins

- 1/4 tsp cream of tartar

Instructions:

1. Preheat oven to 375°F (190°C) and grease 2 (8-oz) ramekins with butter, then dust with granulated sugar.
2. In a medium saucepan over medium heat, melt chocolate and butter together, stirring constantly until smooth.
3. Add flour and whisk until combined.
4. Gradually whisk in milk and cook, stirring constantly, until mixture thickens and comes to a boil. Remove from heat and whisk in egg yolks and 1/4 cup sugar.
5. In a large mixing bowl, beat egg whites and cream of tartar with an electric mixer until stiff peaks form.
6. Gently fold chocolate mixture into egg whites until fully combined.
7. Pour mixture into prepared ramekins and bake for 15-17 minutes, or until soufflés are puffed and set. Serve immediately.

Chocolate Banana Crepes

Ingredients:

- 1 cup all-purpose flour
- 1/4 cup cocoa powder
- 1/4 tsp salt

- 1 1/4 cups milk
- 2 large eggs
- 2 tbsp unsalted butter, melted
- 2 ripe bananas, sliced
- 1/4 cup Nutella, warmed
- Powdered sugar, for dusting

Instructions:

1. In a large mixing bowl, whisk together flour, cocoa powder, and salt.
2. In a separate bowl, whisk together milk, eggs, and melted butter.
3. Gradually whisk wet ingredients into dry ingredients until batter is smooth.
4. Heat a 10-inch nonstick skillet over medium heat. Grease with butter or cooking spray.
5. Pour 1/4 cup of batter into skillet and swirl to coat the bottom. Cook for 1-2 minutes or until crepe is set and edges are slightly browned. Flip and cook for another 30 seconds.
6. Repeat with remaining batter, stacking cooked crepes on a plate.
7. To assemble, spread Nutella on each crepe and top with sliced bananas. Roll up and sprinkle with powdered sugar. Serve immediately.

Chocolate and Hazelnut Tart

Ingredients:

- 1 1/2 cups all-purpose flour
- 1/2 cup unsweetened cocoa powder
- 1/2 teaspoon salt
- 1/2 cup unsalted butter, softened
- 1/2 cup granulated sugar
- 1 large egg
- 1 teaspoon vanilla extract
- 1/4 cup hazelnuts, chopped
- 1/4 cup semisweet chocolate chips
- 1/4 cup heavy cream

Directions:

1. Preheat the oven to 375°F (190°C).
2. In a medium bowl, whisk together the flour, cocoa powder, and salt.
3. In a separate bowl, beat the butter and sugar together until creamy.
4. Add the egg and vanilla extract, and beat until smooth.
5. Gradually add the dry ingredients into the wet mixture, and mix until just combined.
6. Roll the dough into a ball and flatten it into a disc. Wrap the disc in plastic wrap and refrigerate for 30 minutes.
7. After 30 minutes, roll the dough out to 1/4 inch thickness and place it into a 9-inch tart pan. Press the

dough into the bottom and sides of the pan, and trim off any excess dough.

8. Prick the bottom of the dough with a fork and bake for 10-12 minutes, or until the edges start to turn golden brown.

9. Remove the tart from the oven and sprinkle the hazelnuts and chocolate chips over the bottom of the crust.

10. In a small saucepan, heat the heavy cream over low heat until it begins to simmer. Pour the cream over the hazelnuts and chocolate chips.

11. Return the tart to the oven and bake for an additional 10-15 minutes, or until the filling is set.

12. Let the tart cool for 30 minutes before slicing and serving.

Chocolate Covered Strawberries Ice Cream

Ingredients:

- 2 cups heavy cream
- 1 cup whole milk
- 1/2 cup granulated sugar
- 1/2 cup unsweetened cocoa powder
- 1 teaspoon vanilla extract
- 1/2 cup chocolate covered strawberries, chopped

Directions:

1. In a medium saucepan, whisk together the heavy cream, whole milk, sugar, cocoa powder, and vanilla extract.
2. Heat the mixture over medium heat, stirring occasionally, until the sugar has dissolved and the mixture is hot.
3. Remove the pan from the heat and let it cool to room temperature.
4. Pour the mixture into an ice cream maker and churn according to the manufacturer's instructions.
5. When the ice cream is almost done, add the chopped chocolate covered strawberries and let the ice cream machine mix them in.
6. Transfer the ice cream to a freezer-safe container and freeze until firm, at least 4 hours.
7. Serve the ice cream with additional chopped chocolate covered strawberries on top, if desired.

Chocolate and Hazelnut Tart

Ingredients:

- 1 1/4 cups all-purpose flour
- 1/4 cup unsweetened cocoa powder
- 1/2 cup unsalted butter, softened
- 1/2 cup powdered sugar
- 1 large egg yolk

- 1/2 cup hazelnuts, toasted and chopped
- 1 cup semisweet chocolate chips
- 3/4 cup heavy cream

Directions:

1. In a medium bowl, whisk together flour and cocoa powder.
2. In a large bowl, beat butter and powdered sugar until creamy. Add egg yolk and beat until combined.
3. Gradually add flour mixture to butter mixture, stirring until dough forms. Wrap in plastic wrap and refrigerate for at least 30 minutes.
4. Preheat oven to 350°F. Roll out dough and press into a 9-inch tart pan. Prick the bottom of the crust with a fork.
5. Bake for 15 minutes. Let cool completely.
6. In a medium saucepan, heat heavy cream until just boiling. Remove from heat and stir in chocolate chips until melted.
7. Pour chocolate mixture into cooled crust. Top with chopped hazelnuts. Refrigerate for at least 2 hours before serving.

Chocolate Covered Strawberries Ice Cream

Ingredients:

- 2 cups heavy cream
- 1 cup whole milk
- 3/4 cup granulated sugar
- 1/2 cup unsweetened cocoa powder
- 1 tsp vanilla extract
- 1 cup chopped chocolate covered strawberries

Directions:

1. In a large saucepan, whisk together heavy cream, milk, sugar, cocoa powder, and vanilla extract. Heat over medium heat, stirring constantly, until mixture comes to a simmer.
2. Remove from heat and let cool completely.
3. Transfer mixture to an ice cream maker and churn according to manufacturer's instructions.
4. Once ice cream is churned, fold in chopped chocolate covered strawberries.
5. Transfer to a freezer-safe container and freeze for at least 2 hours before serving.

Chocolate and Peanut Butter Banana S'mores

Ingredients:

- 2 ripe bananas, sliced
- 1 cup mini marshmallows
- 1/4 cup peanut butter
- 1/2 cup chocolate chips
- Graham crackers, broken into small pieces

Instructions:

1. Preheat the oven to 350°F (180°C) and line a baking sheet with parchment paper.
2. Arrange the banana slices on the parchment paper, leaving a small space between each slice.
3. In a microwave-safe bowl, melt the peanut butter and chocolate chips together, stirring until smooth.
4. Drizzle the peanut butter and chocolate mixture over the banana slices, then sprinkle the mini marshmallows on top.
5. Bake in the preheated oven for 5-7 minutes, or until the marshmallows are golden brown.
6. Serve with graham crackers for dipping.

Chocolate and Orange Tart with Almond Crust

Ingredients:

For the crust:

- 1 cup almond flour
- 2 tablespoons sugar
- 1/4 teaspoon salt
- 1/4 cup melted butter

For the filling:

- 1 cup heavy cream
- 1/2 cup whole milk
- 2 tablespoons sugar
- Zest of 1 orange
- 6 ounces semisweet chocolate, chopped
- 3 egg yolks
- 1 tablespoon orange liqueur

Instructions:

1. Preheat the oven to 350°F (180°C) and grease a 9-inch tart pan.
2. To make the crust, mix together the almond flour, sugar, and salt in a bowl. Add the melted butter and mix until well combined.

3. Press the mixture into the bottom and up the sides of the prepared tart pan. Bake in the preheated oven for 10-12 minutes, or until golden brown. Let cool completely.

4. In a medium saucepan, heat the cream, milk, sugar, and orange zest over medium heat until just simmering. Remove from heat and stir in the chopped chocolate until melted and smooth.

5. In a separate bowl, whisk together the egg yolks and orange liqueur. Slowly pour the chocolate mixture into the egg mixture, whisking constantly.

6. Pour the filling into the cooled crust and bake in the preheated oven for 25-30 minutes, or until set but still slightly jiggly in the center.

7. Let cool completely before serving. Enjoy!

Chocolate Caramel Brownies

Ingredients:

- 1/2 cup unsalted butter
- 1 cup granulated sugar
- 1/2 cup cocoa powder
- 1/2 teaspoon salt
- 2 eggs
- 1/2 cup all-purpose flour
- 1/2 cup caramel sauce

Instructions:

1. Preheat the oven to 350°F and line an 8-inch square baking pan with parchment paper.
2. Melt the butter in a saucepan over low heat, then add the sugar, cocoa powder, and salt.
3. Stir in the eggs one at a time, then add the flour and mix until smooth.
4. Pour half of the batter into the prepared baking pan and spread it evenly.
5. Pour the caramel sauce over the batter and spread it evenly.
6. Pour the remaining batter over the caramel sauce and spread it evenly.
7. Bake for 25-30 minutes or until a toothpick inserted in the center comes out clean.
8. Let the brownies cool completely in the pan before slicing and serving.

Chocolate Cherry Cheesecake Bars

Ingredients:

- 1 cup all-purpose flour
- 1/2 cup unsalted butter, softened
- 1/4 cup granulated sugar

- 8 oz cream cheese, softened
- 1/4 cup granulated sugar
- 1 egg
- 1/2 teaspoon vanilla extract
- 1/2 cup chocolate chips
- 1/2 cup cherry pie filling

Instructions:

1. Preheat the oven to 350°F and line an 8-inch square baking pan with parchment paper.
2. In a mixing bowl, combine the flour, butter, and sugar and mix until crumbly.
3. Press the mixture into the prepared baking pan to form an even crust.
4. In another mixing bowl, beat the cream cheese and sugar until smooth.
5. Add the egg and vanilla extract and beat until well combined.
6. Fold in the chocolate chips and cherry pie filling.
7. Pour the mixture over the crust and spread it evenly.
8. Bake for 30-35 minutes or until the edges are lightly browned.
9. Let the cheesecake bars cool completely in the pan before slicing and serving.

Chocolate Ganache Tart

Ingredients:

- 1 1/2 cups of all-purpose flour
- 1/4 cup of unsweetened cocoa powder
- 1/4 cup of granulated sugar
- 1/4 tsp of salt
- 1/2 cup of unsalted butter, chilled and cubed
- 1/4 cup of heavy cream
- 8 oz of semisweet chocolate, chopped
- 1/2 cup of heavy cream
- 2 tbsp of unsalted butter

Instructions:

1. Preheat the oven to 350°F (175°C).
2. In a food processor, combine the flour, cocoa powder, sugar, and salt. Pulse a few times to mix.
3. Add the cubed butter to the food processor and pulse until the mixture looks like coarse sand.
4. Add the 1/4 cup of heavy cream and pulse until the dough comes together.
5. Press the dough into the bottom and up the sides of a 9-inch tart pan.
6. Bake for 15-20 minutes, until the crust is set. Let cool completely.
7. Place the chopped chocolate in a heatproof bowl.
8. In a small saucepan, heat the 1/2 cup of heavy cream and 2 tbsp of butter until simmering.

9. Pour the hot cream over the chopped chocolate and let sit for a minute.
10. Whisk the chocolate and cream until smooth.
11. Pour the chocolate ganache into the cooled tart shell.
12. Refrigerate for at least 2 hours, until set.

Chocolate and Peanut Butter Banana Bites

Ingredients:

- 2 ripe bananas
- 1/4 cup of smooth peanut butter
- 4 oz of semisweet chocolate, chopped
- 1 tbsp of coconut oil
- Crushed peanuts (optional)

Instructions:

1. Line a baking sheet with parchment paper.
2. Peel the bananas and cut them into 1-inch slices.
3. Spread a small dollop of peanut butter on each banana slice.
4. Arrange the banana slices on the prepared baking sheet and freeze for 30 minutes.
5. In a small saucepan, melt the chopped chocolate and coconut oil over low heat, stirring constantly.

6. Dip each frozen banana slice into the melted chocolate, using a fork to coat it completely.
7. Place the chocolate-covered banana bites back on the parchment-lined baking sheet.
8. Sprinkle crushed peanuts on top, if desired.
9. Refrigerate for at least 10 minutes, until the chocolate is set. Serve cold.

Chocolate Cherry Almond Clusters

Ingredients:

- 1 cup of semisweet chocolate chips
- 1 cup of dried cherries
- 1 cup of toasted almonds

Instructions:

1. Melt the chocolate chips in a microwave-safe bowl in 30-second intervals, stirring between each interval until fully melted.
2. Stir in the dried cherries and toasted almonds until fully coated.
3. Spoon clusters of the mixture onto a parchment-lined baking sheet.
4. Allow to cool until the chocolate has set.
5. Serve and enjoy!

Chocolate Hazelnut Biscuits

Ingredients:

- 1 cup of all-purpose flour
- 1/2 cup of unsweetened cocoa powder
- 1/2 teaspoon of baking powder
- 1/4 teaspoon of salt
- 1/2 cup of unsalted butter, softened
- 1/2 cup of granulated sugar
- 1 large egg
- 1/2 teaspoon of vanilla extract
- 1/2 cup of chopped hazelnuts

Instructions:

1. Preheat the oven to 350°F and line a baking sheet with parchment paper.
2. In a medium bowl, whisk together the flour, cocoa powder, baking powder, and salt.
3. In a separate large bowl, beat the butter and sugar together until light and fluffy.
4. Beat in the egg and vanilla extract until fully combined.
5. Gradually mix in the dry ingredients until just combined.
6. Fold in the chopped hazelnuts.
7. Roll tablespoon-sized balls of dough and place them on the prepared baking sheet.
8. Bake for 12-15 minutes, or until set.

9. Allow to cool on the baking sheet for a few minutes before transferring to a wire rack to cool completely.
10. Serve and enjoy!

Chocolate Caramel Pecan Bars

Ingredients:

- 1 cup all-purpose flour
- 1/2 cup unsalted butter, melted
- 1/2 cup brown sugar
- 1 cup chopped pecans
- 1 cup semisweet chocolate chips
- 1/2 cup caramel sauce

Instructions:

1. Preheat the oven to 350°F (175°C).
2. In a mixing bowl, combine the flour, melted butter, and brown sugar until crumbly.
3. Press the mixture into an 8x8 inch baking pan and bake for 12-15 minutes until lightly golden.
4. Sprinkle the pecans and chocolate chips over the crust, then drizzle with the caramel sauce.
5. Bake for another 10-12 minutes until the chocolate chips are melted and bubbly.

6. Let the bars cool completely before slicing and serving.

Chocolate Cherry Almond Smoothie Bowl

Ingredients:

- 1 frozen banana
- 1/2 cup frozen cherries
- 1/4 cup unsweetened almond milk
- 1/4 cup unsweetened cocoa powder
- 1 tbsp almond butter
- 1 tbsp honey
- Toppings: sliced almonds, chopped dark chocolate, fresh cherries

Instructions:

1. In a blender, combine the frozen banana, frozen cherries, almond milk, cocoa powder, almond butter, and honey.
2. Blend until smooth and creamy, adding more almond milk if needed.
3. Pour the smoothie into a bowl and top with sliced almonds, chopped dark chocolate, and fresh cherries.
4. Serve immediately and enjoy!

Chocolate Hazelnut Biscotti

Ingredients:

- 2 cups all-purpose flour
- 1/2 cup cocoa powder
- 1 tsp baking powder
- 1/2 tsp salt
- 3 eggs
- 1 cup sugar
- 1/2 cup unsalted butter, melted
- 1 tsp vanilla extract
- 1 cup hazelnuts, chopped

Instructions:

1. Preheat the oven to 350°F.
2. In a medium bowl, whisk together the flour, cocoa powder, baking powder, and salt.
3. In a separate large bowl, beat the eggs and sugar until pale and fluffy.
4. Add the melted butter and vanilla extract to the egg mixture and mix well.
5. Gradually fold in the dry ingredients until a dough forms.
6. Stir in the chopped hazelnuts.
7. Divide the dough in half and shape each half into a log, about 12 inches long and 2 inches wide.
8. Bake the logs on a lined baking sheet for 25-30 minutes, or until firm to the touch.

9. Remove the logs from the oven and let cool for 10 minutes. Reduce the oven temperature to 325°F.
10. Use a serrated knife to slice the logs diagonally into 1/2 inch-thick slices.
11. Place the slices back on the baking sheet and bake for an additional 10-12 minutes, or until crisp.
12. Let the biscotti cool completely before serving.

Chocolate Covered Strawberry Cheesecake Bites

Ingredients:

- 1 package cream cheese, softened
- 1/4 cup sugar
- 1 egg
- 1/2 tsp vanilla extract
- 12 strawberries, hulled
- 1/2 cup semi-sweet chocolate chips
- 1 tsp coconut oil

Instructions:

1. Preheat the oven to 350°F. Line a muffin tin with 12 paper liners.
2. In a large bowl, beat the cream cheese and sugar until smooth.

3. Add the egg and vanilla extract to the cream cheese mixture and mix well.
4. Spoon the mixture evenly into the paper liners, filling each about 2/3 full.
5. Place one strawberry in the center of each muffin cup, pressing it lightly into the cream cheese mixture.
6. Bake for 20-25 minutes, or until the cheesecake is set and slightly golden.
7. Remove the cheesecake bites from the muffin tin and let cool completely on a wire rack.
8. In a small microwave-safe bowl, melt the chocolate chips and coconut oil in 30-second intervals, stirring after each interval, until smooth.
9. Dip each cheesecake bite into the melted chocolate, covering the strawberry completely.
10. Place the chocolate-covered bites on a lined baking sheet and refrigerate until the chocolate is set, about 30 minutes.
11. Serve chilled.

Chocolate Hazelnut Cake

Ingredients:

- 1 1/2 cups all-purpose flour
- 3/4 cup unsweetened cocoa powder
- 1 1/2 teaspoons baking powder

- 1 teaspoon baking soda
- 1/2 teaspoon salt
- 1 1/2 cups granulated sugar
- 1/2 cup vegetable oil
- 2 large eggs
- 1 teaspoon vanilla extract
- 1 cup milk
- 1 cup hazelnut spread

Directions:

1. Preheat oven to 350°F (180°C) and grease a 9-inch cake pan.
2. In a medium bowl, whisk together flour, cocoa powder, baking powder, baking soda, and salt.
3. In a large bowl, beat together sugar, oil, eggs, and vanilla until creamy.
4. Gradually add flour mixture and milk to the sugar mixture, alternating between the two.
5. Pour half of the batter into the prepared cake pan.
6. Drop spoonfuls of hazelnut spread onto the batter.
7. Pour the remaining batter on top of the hazelnut spread.
8. Bake for 35-40 minutes, or until a toothpick inserted in the center comes out clean.
9. Allow the cake to cool before serving.

Chocolate and Raspberry Tart

Ingredients:

- 1 1/2 cups all-purpose flour
- 1/2 cup unsalted butter, chilled and cubed
- 1/4 cup granulated sugar
- 1 large egg yolk
- 1/4 cup raspberry jam
- 1/4 cup heavy cream
- 8 ounces semisweet chocolate, chopped
- 1/4 cup fresh raspberries

Directions:

1. Preheat oven to 350°F (180°C).
2. In a food processor, pulse together flour, butter, and sugar until crumbly.
3. Add egg yolk and pulse until a dough forms.
4. Press the dough into a 9-inch tart pan with a removable bottom.
5. Spread raspberry jam evenly over the dough.
6. Bake for 20-25 minutes, or until the crust is golden brown.
7. In a small saucepan, heat the heavy cream until it comes to a simmer.
8. Remove from heat and add chopped chocolate.
9. Whisk until the chocolate is melted and the mixture is smooth.
10. Pour the chocolate mixture into the crust.

11. Refrigerate for at least 2 hours, or until set.

12. Top with fresh raspberries before serving.

Chocolate Coconut Macadamia Nut Bars

Ingredients:

- 1 cup unsweetened shredded coconut
- 1/2 cup raw macadamia nuts, chopped
- 1/2 cup almond flour
- 1/4 cup coconut oil, melted
- 1/4 cup pure maple syrup
- 1/4 cup cocoa powder
- 1 tsp pure vanilla extract
- Pinch of sea salt

Instructions:

1. Preheat the oven to 350°F.
2. In a bowl, mix together the coconut, macadamia nuts, and almond flour.
3. Add in the melted coconut oil, maple syrup, cocoa powder, vanilla extract, and sea salt. Stir until well combined.
4. Press the mixture into an 8-inch square baking dish.

5. Bake for 15-20 minutes or until the edges are golden brown.
6. Let cool before slicing into bars.

Chocolate Banana Oat Cookies

Ingredients:

- 2 ripe bananas, mashed
- 1 cup rolled oats
- 1/4 cup cocoa powder
- 1/4 cup chocolate chips
- 1 tsp pure vanilla extract
- Pinch of sea salt

Instructions:

1. Preheat the oven to 350°F.
2. In a bowl, mix together the mashed bananas, rolled oats, cocoa powder, chocolate chips, vanilla extract, and sea salt.
3. Drop spoonfuls of the mixture onto a baking sheet lined with parchment paper.
4. Bake for 12-15 minutes or until the edges are firm and the tops are slightly cracked.
5. Let cool before serving.

Chocolate Toffee Crunch Bark

Ingredients:

- 1 pound dark chocolate, chopped
- 1 cup toffee bits
- 1/4 cup chopped roasted almonds

Instructions:

1. Line a baking sheet with parchment paper.
2. Melt the chopped chocolate in a double boiler or in the microwave, stirring every 30 seconds until melted and smooth.
3. Spread the melted chocolate on the parchment paper, making an even layer about 1/4 inch thick.
4. Sprinkle the toffee bits and chopped almonds over the melted chocolate.
5. Place the baking sheet in the refrigerator for about 20 minutes or until the chocolate has hardened.
6. Once the chocolate has hardened, break the bark into pieces and serve.

Chocolate Cream Pie

Ingredients:

- 1 1/4 cups all-purpose flour
- 1/4 teaspoon salt
- 1/2 cup unsalted butter, chilled and cubed
- 3 tablespoons cold water
- 1 cup heavy cream
- 1/2 cup whole milk
- 2/3 cup granulated sugar
- 1/4 cup cornstarch
- 1/4 teaspoon salt
- 4 egg yolks
- 6 ounces semisweet chocolate, chopped
- 1 tablespoon unsalted butter
- 1 teaspoon vanilla extract

Directions:

1. Preheat oven to 375°F.
2. In a large mixing bowl, whisk together flour and salt. Add butter and use a pastry cutter or your hands to cut the butter into the flour until the mixture resembles coarse sand.
3. Add water, 1 tablespoon at a time, until the dough comes together in a ball. Flatten the dough into a disk, wrap in plastic wrap, and refrigerate for at least 30 minutes.
4. Roll out the dough on a floured surface to fit a 9-inch pie dish. Trim the edges and prick the bottom of the crust

with a fork. Bake for 12-15 minutes or until lightly golden brown.

5. In a saucepan over medium heat, combine cream, milk, sugar, cornstarch, and salt. Whisk until smooth. Add egg yolks and whisk until combined.

6. Add chocolate and butter, stirring until melted and smooth. Remove from heat and stir in vanilla extract.

7. Pour the filling into the crust and smooth the top. Chill in the refrigerator for at least 2 hours or until set.

Chocolate Raspberry Torte

Ingredients:

- 1 cup all-purpose flour
- 1/2 cup unsweetened cocoa powder
- 1/2 teaspoon baking soda
- 1/4 teaspoon salt
- 1/2 cup unsalted butter, softened
- 1 cup granulated sugar
- 2 large eggs
- 1/2 cup sour cream
- 1/2 cup raspberry jam
- 1/2 cup semisweet chocolate chips
- 1/4 cup heavy cream
- Fresh raspberries, for garnish

Directions:

1. Preheat oven to 350°F. Grease and flour a 9-inch springform pan.
2. In a medium mixing bowl, whisk together flour, cocoa powder, baking soda, and salt.
3. In a large mixing bowl, beat butter and sugar together until light and fluffy. Add eggs, one at a time, beating well after each addition.
4. Add sour cream and mix until combined.
5. Gradually add the flour mixture, mixing until just combined.
6. Pour batter into the prepared pan and smooth the top. Bake for 30-35 minutes or until a toothpick inserted into the center comes out clean. Allow to cool completely.
7. Spread raspberry jam on top of the torte.
8. In a microwave-safe bowl, heat chocolate chips and heavy cream in 20-second intervals, stirring after each interval, until melted and smooth.
9. Pour the chocolate over the raspberry jam and spread evenly. Chill in the refrigerator for at least 1 hour or until the chocolate is set.
10. Garnish with fresh raspberries before serving.

Chocolate Lovers' Tart

Ingredients:

- 1 1/2 cups all-purpose flour
- 1/2 cup unsalted butter, chilled and cubed
- 1/4 cup granulated sugar
- 1/4 cup unsweetened cocoa powder
- 1/4 tsp salt
- 1 large egg
- 1/2 cup semisweet chocolate chips
- 1/2 cup heavy cream
- 1 tbsp unsalted butter
- 1/4 cup confectioners' sugar
- 1/4 cup chopped nuts (optional)

Instructions:

1. Preheat oven to 350°F (180°C). Grease a 9-inch tart pan with removable bottom.
2. In a food processor, pulse together flour, butter, granulated sugar, cocoa powder, and salt until mixture resembles coarse sand.
3. Add egg and pulse until dough comes together.
4. Press dough into bottom and up sides of prepared pan.
5. Bake for 20 minutes or until firm to the touch.
6. In a saucepan over medium heat, melt chocolate chips, heavy cream, and butter until smooth.
7. Remove from heat and stir in confectioners' sugar.

8. Pour chocolate mixture into tart shell and sprinkle with nuts, if using.
9. Chill in refrigerator for at least 2 hours before serving.

Double Chocolate Chip Cookies

Ingredients:

- 1 cup all-purpose flour
- 1/2 cup unsweetened cocoa powder
- 1 tsp baking soda
- 1/2 tsp salt
- 1/2 cup unsalted butter, at room temperature
- 1/2 cup granulated sugar
- 1/2 cup light brown sugar
- 1 large egg
- 1 tsp vanilla extract
- 1/2 cup semisweet chocolate chips
- 1/2 cup milk chocolate chips

Instructions:

1. Preheat oven to 350°F (180°C). Line a baking sheet with parchment paper.
2. In a medium bowl, whisk together flour, cocoa powder, baking soda, and salt.

3. In a separate large bowl, beat butter, granulated sugar, and brown sugar until light and fluffy.

4. Beat in egg and vanilla extract until well combined.

5. Gradually stir in flour mixture until just combined.

6. Stir in chocolate chips.

7. Roll dough into 1-inch balls and place onto prepared baking sheet.

8. Bake for 10-12 minutes or until edges are set.

9. Let cookies cool on baking sheet for 5 minutes before transferring to a wire rack to cool completely.

Chocolate Fudge Cake

Ingredients:

- 2 cups all-purpose flour
- 2 cups granulated sugar
- ¾ cup unsweetened cocoa powder
- 2 teaspoons baking soda
- 1 teaspoon baking powder
- 1 teaspoon salt
- 1 cup vegetable oil
- 1 cup buttermilk
- 2 large eggs
- 2 teaspoons vanilla extract
- **1 cup hot water**

- 1 cup semisweet chocolate chips

Directions:

1. Preheat the oven to 350°F (180°C). Grease and flour a 9-inch (23cm) cake pan.
2. In a large mixing bowl, whisk together flour, sugar, cocoa powder, baking soda, baking powder, and salt.
3. Add oil, buttermilk, eggs, and vanilla extract to the dry ingredients and whisk until smooth.
4. Gradually add hot water to the batter and whisk until well combined.
5. Fold in chocolate chips.
6. Pour the batter into the prepared pan and bake for 30-35 minutes, or until a toothpick inserted into the center of the cake comes out clean.
7. Let the cake cool in the pan for 10 minutes, then remove from the pan and transfer to a wire rack to cool completely.
8. Dust with powdered sugar or decorate with your favorite frosting.

Chocolate Caramel Cheesecake Bars

Ingredients:

- 1 ½ cups all-purpose flour
- ⅓ cup granulated sugar
- ⅓ cup brown sugar
- 1 teaspoon baking powder
- ¼ teaspoon salt
- ½ cup unsalted butter, softened
- 1 large egg
- 1 teaspoon vanilla extract
- 1 (8-ounce) package cream cheese, softened
- ½ cup granulated sugar
- 1 large egg
- 1 teaspoon vanilla extract
- ½ cup semisweet chocolate chips
- ½ cup caramel sauce

Directions:

1. Preheat the oven to 350°F (180°C). Grease and flour a 9-inch (23cm) square baking pan.
2. In a medium mixing bowl, whisk together flour, granulated sugar, brown sugar, baking powder, and salt.
3. Cut in butter with a pastry blender until the mixture is crumbly.

4. Add egg and vanilla extract to the mixture and mix until the dough comes together.
5. Press the dough evenly into the bottom of the prepared pan.
6. In a large mixing bowl, beat cream cheese until creamy.
7. Gradually add granulated sugar, egg, and vanilla extract, beating until smooth.
8. Fold in chocolate chips.
9. Pour the cream cheese mixture over the dough in the pan and spread evenly.
10. Drizzle caramel sauce over the cream cheese mixture.
11. Bake for 30-35 minutes, or until the edges are lightly browned and the center is set.
12. Let cool in the pan for 10 minutes, then transfer to a wire rack to cool completely.
13. Cut into bars and serve.

Chocolate Cherry Galette

Ingredients:

- 1 sheet of frozen puff pastry, thawed
- 2 cups of pitted cherries
- 1/4 cup of granulated sugar
- 1 tablespoon of cornstarch
- 1/2 teaspoon of vanilla extract

- 1/2 cup of semisweet chocolate chips
- 1 egg, beaten
- Coarse sugar, for sprinkling

Instructions:

1. Preheat the oven to 400°F (205°C).
2. In a large bowl, toss the cherries with the sugar, cornstarch, and vanilla extract.
3. Roll out the puff pastry on a lightly floured surface and place it on a parchment-lined baking sheet.
4. Sprinkle the chocolate chips in the center of the pastry.
5. Add the cherry mixture on top of the chocolate chips, leaving a 1-inch border.
6. Fold the edges of the pastry over the filling, pleating as you go.
7. Brush the edges of the pastry with the beaten egg and sprinkle with coarse sugar.
8. Bake for 25-30 minutes or until the pastry is golden brown and the filling is bubbling.
9. Let cool for 5 minutes before serving.

Chocolate Hazelnut Crunch

Ingredients:

- 1 cup of hazelnuts, chopped

- 1 cup of semisweet chocolate chips
- 1/2 cup of heavy cream
- 1/4 cup of unsalted butter
- 1/4 cup of light corn syrup
- 1/4 teaspoon of salt
- 1 teaspoon of vanilla extract

Instructions:

1. Preheat the oven to 350°F (175°C).
2. Spread the chopped hazelnuts on a baking sheet and toast for 8-10 minutes or until golden brown.
3. In a saucepan, combine the chocolate chips, heavy cream, butter, corn syrup, and salt over medium heat.
4. Stir until the chocolate is melted and the mixture is smooth.
5. Remove from the heat and stir in the vanilla extract and toasted hazelnuts.
6. Pour the mixture into an 8x8 inch baking dish lined with parchment paper.
7. Smooth the top with a spatula and chill in the refrigerator for at least 2 hours or until firm.
8. Remove the chocolate from the baking dish and cut into small squares.
9. Serve chilled or at room temperature.

Chocolate Covered Banana Bites

Ingredients:

- 2 ripe bananas
- 1 cup semisweet chocolate chips
- 1 tablespoon coconut oil
- Toppings of your choice (crushed nuts, shredded coconut, sprinkles, etc.)

Instructions:

1. Peel the bananas and cut them into bite-sized pieces.
2. Melt the chocolate chips and coconut oil in a microwave-safe bowl or over a double boiler.
3. Dip the banana pieces into the melted chocolate, making sure they are fully coated.
4. Place the chocolate-covered bananas onto a parchment-lined baking sheet and sprinkle with your desired toppings.
5. Refrigerate for at least 30 minutes or until the chocolate has hardened.
6. Serve and enjoy!

Chocolate Peanut Butter Granola Bars

Ingredients:

- 2 cups rolled oats
- 1/2 cup peanut butter
- 1/4 cup honey
- 1/4 cup unsweetened cocoa powder
- 1/4 cup dark chocolate chips
- 1/4 cup chopped peanuts

Instructions:

1. Preheat the oven to 350°F (180°C) and line a 9x9-inch baking dish with parchment paper.
2. In a large bowl, mix together the rolled oats, peanut butter, honey, and cocoa powder until well combined.
3. Fold in the chocolate chips and chopped peanuts.
4. Press the mixture into the prepared baking dish and bake for 15-20 minutes or until the edges are golden brown.
5. Allow the granola bars to cool completely before cutting into squares.
6. Serve and enjoy!

Chocolate Cherry Cheesecake Bars with Oat Crust

Ingredients:

- 1 1/2 cups rolled oats
- 1/2 cup all-purpose flour
- 1/2 cup brown sugar
- 1/4 teaspoon salt
- 1/2 cup unsalted butter, melted
- 8 ounces cream cheese, at room temperature
- 1/3 cup granulated sugar
- 1 large egg
- 1 teaspoon pure vanilla extract
- 1/2 cup dark chocolate chips
- 1/2 cup chopped fresh cherries

Instructions:

1. Preheat the oven to 350°F (175°C). Line an 8-inch square baking dish with parchment paper.
2. In a large bowl, mix together the rolled oats, all-purpose flour, brown sugar, and salt. Stir in the melted butter until the mixture is crumbly.
3. Press the mixture into the bottom of the prepared baking dish, and bake for 10 minutes.
4. Meanwhile, in a separate bowl, beat the cream cheese and granulated sugar until smooth. Beat in the egg and vanilla extract.
5. Stir in the dark chocolate chips and chopped cherries.

6. Pour the cheesecake mixture over the partially baked crust and smooth the top.
7. Bake for 20 to 25 minutes, or until the cheesecake is set and lightly golden.
8. Let cool completely in the baking dish, then chill in the refrigerator for at least 2 hours before slicing into bars.

Chocolate Hazelnut Brownie Bites

Ingredients:

- 1/2 cup unsalted butter
- 1/2 cup granulated sugar
- 1/2 cup all-purpose flour
- 1/4 cup unsweetened cocoa powder
- 1/4 teaspoon salt
- 2 large eggs
- 1 teaspoon pure vanilla extract
- 1/2 cup chopped hazelnuts
- 1/2 cup semisweet chocolate chips

Instructions:

1. Preheat the oven to 350°F (175°C). Grease a mini muffin tin.

2. In a medium saucepan, melt the butter over medium heat. Remove from heat and stir in the granulated sugar until well combined.
3. Stir in the flour, cocoa powder, and salt until smooth.
4. Beat in the eggs and vanilla extract until well combined.
5. Stir in the chopped hazelnuts and semisweet chocolate chips.
6. Spoon the batter into the prepared muffin tin, filling each cup about 3/4 full.
7. Bake for 12 to 15 minutes, or until a toothpick inserted in the center of a brownie bite comes out clean.
8. Let cool in the muffin tin for 5 minutes, then transfer to a wire rack to cool completely. Serve at room temperature.

Chocolate Panna Cotta

Ingredients:

- 2 cups heavy cream
- 1/2 cup granulated sugar
- 1/4 cup unsweetened cocoa powder
- 1/4 tsp salt
- 1/4 cup water
- 2 1/4 tsp unflavored gelatin
- 1 tsp vanilla extract
- Whipped cream and shaved chocolate for garnish

Directions:

1. In a medium saucepan, whisk together heavy cream, sugar, cocoa powder, and salt over medium heat. Bring to a simmer, stirring constantly.
2. Meanwhile, in a small bowl, sprinkle gelatin over water and let it sit for 5 minutes.
3. Add the gelatin mixture to the cream mixture and whisk until dissolved.
4. Remove from heat and stir in vanilla extract.
5. Pour the mixture into 6 ramekins or glasses and chill in the refrigerator for at least 3 hours or until set.
6. Serve with whipped cream and shaved chocolate on top.

Chocolate Chip Cookie Cheesecake Bars

Ingredients:

- 1 cup all-purpose flour
- 1/2 cup unsalted butter, softened
- 1/4 cup granulated sugar
- 1/2 tsp vanilla extract
- 1/4 tsp salt
- 8 oz cream cheese, softened
- 1/2 cup granulated sugar
- 1 large egg
- 1/2 tsp vanilla extract

- 1/2 cup semisweet chocolate chips

Directions:

1. Preheat oven to 350°F (180°C). Grease a 9-inch square baking pan.
2. In a medium bowl, whisk together flour and salt. In a large bowl, cream together butter, sugar, and vanilla extract until light and fluffy. Add flour mixture and mix until well combined.
3. Press the dough evenly onto the bottom of the prepared pan. Bake for 10-12 minutes or until the edges are lightly golden.
4. In a large bowl, beat cream cheese and sugar until smooth. Beat in egg and vanilla extract until well combined. Fold in chocolate chips.
5. Pour the cream cheese mixture over the cookie base and smooth the top.
6. Bake for 25-30 minutes or until the cheesecake layer is set.
7. Cool the bars completely in the pan, then chill in the refrigerator for at least 1 hour before slicing into bars.

Chocolate Avocado Mousse

Ingredients:

- 2 ripe avocados
- 1/2 cup unsweetened cocoa powder
- 1/2 cup maple syrup
- 1/4 cup almond milk
- 1 tsp vanilla extract
- Pinch of salt
- Optional toppings: whipped cream, chopped nuts, fresh berries

Instructions:

1. Cut avocados in half, remove pit, and scoop flesh into a blender or food processor.
2. Add cocoa powder, maple syrup, almond milk, vanilla extract, and salt to the blender/food processor.
3. Blend until smooth and creamy, scraping down the sides as needed.
4. Spoon mixture into dessert bowls or ramekins and refrigerate for at least 30 minutes or until set.
5. When ready to serve, top with whipped cream, chopped nuts, or fresh berries.

Chocolate Oatmeal Bars

Ingredients:

- 2 cups rolled oats
- 1/2 cup almond flour
- 1/4 cup cocoa powder
- 1/4 cup honey
- 1/4 cup coconut oil
- 1/4 cup almond butter
- 1 tsp vanilla extract
- 1/4 tsp salt
- Optional toppings: chocolate chips, chopped nuts, dried fruit

Instructions:

1. Preheat oven to 350°F (175°C) and line an 8-inch square baking dish with parchment paper.
2. In a large mixing bowl, combine oats, almond flour, cocoa powder, and salt.
3. In a separate bowl, melt together honey, coconut oil, almond butter, and vanilla extract in the microwave or on the stovetop.
4. Pour the wet mixture over the dry mixture and stir until well combined.
5. Press mixture evenly into the bottom of the prepared baking dish.
6. Bake for 18-20 minutes or until the edges start to pull away from the sides of the dish.

7. Let cool for at least 10 minutes before cutting into bars.

8. Optional: top bars with chocolate chips, chopped nuts, or dried fruit before serving.

Chocolate Pudding Cake

Ingredients:

- 1 cup all-purpose flour
- 2 teaspoons baking powder
- 1/4 teaspoon salt
- 1/2 cup granulated sugar
- 1/4 cup unsweetened cocoa powder
- 1/2 cup milk
- 2 tablespoons vegetable oil
- 1 teaspoon vanilla extract
- 1/2 cup semisweet chocolate chips
- 1 cup hot water

Instructions:

1. Preheat oven to 350°F.
2. In a medium bowl, whisk together flour, baking powder, salt, sugar, and cocoa powder.
3. Add milk, vegetable oil, and vanilla extract to the dry ingredients and mix until smooth.
4. Stir in chocolate chips.

5. Pour batter into an 8-inch square baking dish.

6. Sprinkle hot water over the batter. Do not stir.

7. Bake for 30-35 minutes, until the top of the cake is set.

8. Let cool for 10 minutes before serving. Serve with whipped cream or ice cream, if desired.

Chocolate Cherry Cupcakes

Ingredients:

- 1 1/2 cups all-purpose flour
- 1/2 cup unsweetened cocoa powder
- 1 teaspoon baking powder
- 1/2 teaspoon baking soda
- 1/4 teaspoon salt
- 1/2 cup unsalted butter, softened
- 1 cup granulated sugar
- 2 large eggs
- 1 teaspoon vanilla extract
- 1/2 cup milk
- 1 cup chopped fresh cherries

Instructions:

1. Preheat oven to 350°F. Line a muffin tin with paper liners.

2. In a medium bowl, whisk together flour, cocoa powder, baking powder, baking soda, and salt.
3. In a large bowl, cream together butter and sugar until light and fluffy.
4. Add eggs, one at a time, beating well after each addition.
5. Mix in vanilla extract.
6. Add flour mixture and milk alternately to the butter mixture, beginning and ending with the flour mixture. Mix until just combined.
7. Stir in chopped cherries.
8. Divide batter evenly among muffin cups.
9. Bake for 20-25 minutes, until a toothpick inserted into the center of a cupcake comes out clean.
10. Let cool in the pan for 5 minutes, then transfer to a wire rack to cool completely. Frost with your favorite frosting, if desired.

Chocolate and Raspberry Mousse

Ingredients:

- 1 cup of fresh raspberries
- 2 tbsp of sugar
- 1/2 cup of heavy cream
- 1/2 cup of dark chocolate chips
- 1 egg white

- 1/4 tsp of cream of tartar

Instructions:

1. In a small saucepan, mix the raspberries and sugar together and cook over medium heat until the sugar dissolves and the raspberries break down.
2. Strain the mixture through a fine mesh strainer to remove the seeds and set aside to cool.
3. In a separate bowl, beat the egg white and cream of tartar until stiff peaks form.
4. Melt the chocolate chips in a double boiler or in the microwave, stirring until smooth.
5. In a third bowl, beat the heavy cream until it forms soft peaks.
6. Mix the melted chocolate into the raspberry puree and fold in the beaten egg white and whipped cream.
7. Divide the mousse into individual serving cups and chill for at least 2 hours.

Chocolate and Almond Biscotti

Ingredients:

- 2 cups of all-purpose flour
- 3/4 cup of sugar

- 1/2 cup of unsweetened cocoa powder
- 1 tsp of baking soda
- 1/4 tsp of salt
- 3 eggs
- 1 tsp of vanilla extract
- 1/2 cup of sliced almonds

Instructions:

1. Preheat the oven to 350°F and line a baking sheet with parchment paper.
2. In a large mixing bowl, combine the flour, sugar, cocoa powder, baking soda, and salt.
3. In a separate bowl, whisk together the eggs and vanilla extract.
4. Add the egg mixture to the dry ingredients and stir until a stiff dough forms.
5. Mix in the sliced almonds.
6. On a floured surface, divide the dough into two equal parts and shape each into a long, flattened log.
7. Bake the logs on the prepared baking sheet for 25 minutes or until firm.
8. Remove the logs from the oven and let them cool for 10 minutes before slicing into 1/2-inch thick pieces.
9. Arrange the biscotti slices on the baking sheet and bake for an additional 15-20 minutes or until crisp and dry.

Chocolate Toffee Crunch Bars

Ingredients:

- 2 cups of semisweet chocolate chips
- 1 cup of toffee bits
- 1/4 cup of heavy cream
- 1/4 cup of unsalted butter
- 1/4 teaspoon of salt
- 1/2 cup of chopped almonds

Directions:

1. Line an 8x8 inch baking pan with parchment paper.
2. In a microwave-safe bowl, combine the chocolate chips, heavy cream, and unsalted butter.
3. Microwave on high for 30 seconds, then stir. Continue to microwave in 15-second increments until the chocolate is fully melted and smooth.
4. Stir in the salt and 3/4 cup of the toffee bits.
5. Pour the mixture into the prepared pan and spread evenly.
6. Sprinkle the chopped almonds and remaining 1/4 cup of toffee bits on top.
7. Chill in the refrigerator for 1 hour, or until firm.
8. Cut into bars and serve.

Chocolate Banana Split

Ingredients:

- 2 ripe bananas, sliced
- 1/2 cup of semisweet chocolate chips
- 2 tablespoons of heavy cream
- 1/4 cup of chopped peanuts
- 1/4 cup of maraschino cherries
- Whipped cream

Directions:

1. In a microwave-safe bowl, combine the chocolate chips and heavy cream.
2. Microwave on high for 30 seconds, then stir. Continue to microwave in 15-second increments until the chocolate is fully melted and smooth.
3. Arrange the sliced bananas in a bowl or on a plate.
4. Drizzle the melted chocolate over the bananas.
5. Sprinkle the chopped peanuts and maraschino cherries on top.
6. Add a dollop of whipped cream.
7. Serve immediately.

Chocolate and Pistachio Cake

Ingredients:

- 1 1/2 cups all-purpose flour
- 1/2 cup unsweetened cocoa powder
- 1 tsp baking powder
- 1/2 tsp baking soda
- 1/2 tsp salt
- 1/2 cup unsalted butter, softened
- 1 cup granulated sugar
- 2 large eggs
- 1 tsp vanilla extract
- 1 cup milk
- 1/2 cup chopped pistachios
- 1/2 cup chocolate chips

Instructions:

1. Preheat oven to 350°F (175°C). Grease a 9-inch round cake pan.
2. In a medium bowl, whisk together flour, cocoa powder, baking powder, baking soda, and salt.
3. In a large bowl, cream butter and sugar until light and fluffy.
4. Beat in eggs, one at a time, then stir in vanilla.
5. Gradually add flour mixture to butter mixture, alternating with milk, and beating well after each addition.

6. Fold in chopped pistachios and chocolate chips.
7. Pour batter into prepared pan and smooth top.
8. Bake for 30-35 minutes or until a toothpick inserted in the center comes out clean.
9. Let cool in pan for 10 minutes before removing and placing on a wire rack to cool completely.

Chocolate and Raspberry Trifle

Ingredients:

- 1 box chocolate cake mix, prepared according to package instructions
- 1 1/2 cups heavy cream
- 1/4 cup granulated sugar
- 1 tsp vanilla extract
- 1 pint fresh raspberries
- 1/2 cup raspberry jam
- 1/2 cup chocolate shavings

Instructions:

1. Bake the chocolate cake according to package instructions and let cool completely.
2. In a large bowl, beat heavy cream, sugar, and vanilla extract until stiff peaks form.

3. Cut the chocolate cake into small cubes.
4. In a trifle dish, layer the chocolate cake, raspberry jam, fresh raspberries, and whipped cream.
5. Repeat the layering until all ingredients are used, ending with a layer of whipped cream on top.
6. Sprinkle chocolate shavings over the top layer of whipped cream.
7. Chill in the refrigerator for at least 2 hours before serving.